THE WIND AND THE RAIN

First published in 2023 by Blue Diode Press
30 Lochend Road
Leith
Edinburgh EH6 8BS
www.bluediode.co.uk

All rights reserved. No part of this book may be reproduced, stored in a retrieval system, or transmitted in any form, or by any means, electronic, mechanical, photocopying, recording or otherwise, without prior written permission from Blue Diode Press.

Copyright © Anthony Wilson, 2023

The right of Anthony Wilson to be identified as author of this work has been asserted in accordance with Section 77 of the Copyright, Designs and Patents Act 1988.

ISBN: 978-1-9164051-3-4

Typesetting: Rob A. Mackenzie.
text in Pilgrim LT Roman.

Cover art: Lucy Runge
Cover design: Rob A. Mackenzie

Diode logo design: Sam and Ian Alexander.

Printed and bound by Imprint Digital, Exeter, UK.
https://digital.imprint.co.uk

THE WIND AND THE RAIN

Anthony Wilson

BLUE DIODE PRESS
Edinburgh

In memory of my mother

•

The Ghost-Tree

How long since the willow went?
On quiet days her laughter ripples there,
the piles of dead leaves frittering.

•

There will come a time when people
decide you've had enough of your grief,
and they'll try to take it away from you.

—*Sarah Manguso*, *300 Arguments*

Contents

9	Train
10	To My Rain
13	Waking the Dead
14	After Raymond Carver
15	Before the Frost
17	Body
20	Units
22	Call Me
23	Wall
24	You Were Good
25	Mother/Son
34	Hymn of Rain
35	All There
36	Truce
37	The Divide
38	Fury
39	The Small Rain
42	To the Wife of a Famous Poet
44	The Gift of Tongues
45	Sorry
46	With Hey, Ho, the Wind and the Rain
50	Old School
56	In Late Rainy Season
57	It Raineth
60	Bowled
61	Illusion IV (part of a series)
62	All is Lost (Spoiler Alert)
64	Now and Not Yet
65	On the Nature of Daylight
66	Toast
67	I Mean to Call Daddy
68	Piste Vita

Train

Like this train
heading west

through rain
I travel into it

learning about loss
as I go.

Last night my father
conked out in his chair –

he has so much
to think about –

which is what I have just done
Pewsey, Westbury, Castle Cary

floating by
in a dream

a very grey dream.
You only need to visit Venice once

because it never leaves you.
At Paddington

my flat white was not flat
nor was it white.

To My Rain

1.

Like the poet
who asked me at a party

if she should have heard of me
if you need to know what these poems

are about
you aren't really interested.

Of all the Swiss poets
living in Exeter

I'm the most obsessed
with rain

because when I wake up
each day

the rain's there
even when it's not raining.

What more
do you want?

When Peggy Ashcroft said
'There was a nail'

to explain why her Chagall
hung behind a spare bedroom door –

that's how I feel
about the rain.

2.

I am falling
pretty much

continuously
and in stair-rods.

That I manage this
without crying

is my secret
one that leads to more tears

at a date of my choosing
(I mean, my body's –

it always knows best).
Apparently, I never make a point

in a meeting
without first touching my face.

I'm touching it now
as I lean over this notebook

a brilliant day in March
(I can't believe I'm saying this)

with no rain.
If I knew

how to fall
silently

don't you think
I would have perfected it

by now?

Waking the Dead

We watch a lot of death.
No wonder we're exhausted.
The lead actor with a Shakespearean pedigree
looks closer to breaking down in each episode.
It's the minor roles I feel sorry for.
Those who went to less-grand schools,
forever typecast as Evil Scot 2
or Psychopath with Midlands Accent.
You can see them working as hard as the pretty ones –
just to keep the camera interested.
Then the lens drifts back to its real preoccupation,
namely how a man (it is always a man)
can witness so much death, eat and shave so terribly,
and still retain decency towards those around him,
those poor colleagues and relatives he shouts at,
banging the table for no apparent reason
other than they mentioned Agatha Christie.

After Raymond Carver

Did I sleep that time?
You know I did. I did nothing else. Just not at night.
Those documentaries about Transit vans.
All those *Frasiers* all those *Will and Grace*s.
School, too. The run to breakfast.
Exercise, before eating!
The punishments. Running as punishment.
I walk now, with the dog. I walk into it.
I want to disappear into
'the early morning stuff which passes for thought'.
The same for my mother.
Not as she was, but as she was.
The laughter, the elegance, the smell of onions frying.
How did she do it? She never stopped.
Early mornings, before anyone's up.
Today. November. Actually black.
Not 'dark', but black.
I walked into it. I walk into it.

Before the Frost

   1.

'He asked me had I been saved. I told him I had.'
Cut to Wallander pacing the woods, the shack surrounded.
A steel trap wraps round his foot. Everyone opens fire.

Next he's shovelling painkillers,
his lieutenant reading from the Bible passages
plastered onto the walls.
'Do you know where this church is?'

Now he's being followed on the way back to his car.
The reverse camera angle says
everything we need to know.

   2.

Symphony of crying voices.
'They're easier to get hold of than you think.'
     'She was upset.'
'She's done it before. You know she's done it before.'
They stand across the kitchen from each other,
the years and failure of their parenting
catching up with them in white space.

   3.

In the moment Linda tells him she's pregnant,
a black cross hangs on the wall between them.
Barely time for this to register before
the inevitable car chase, in which
 two Volvos advertise their speed for free.

When they argue later about why she didn't invite him to her wedding,
it's the same room in which, in the final series, they discuss his dementia.

Body

1.

It took me a long time
to realise I was a body.
Am a body.
I was all packed lunches and uphill gears.
Never once did I stop to breathe
or let myself acknowledge pain.
I want to wake up and be healed.
I know I'll wake up without healing.
Me, here, this body.
The one it took me years to admit to.
The one that's dying, as it heals
and breathes here in the dark.

2.

Is this prayer?
Is this a kind of prayer,
to sit in silence for the first time
after a long day of emails and meetings
and come back to breath,
come back to nothing but my breath
in the dark room,
the dog snuffling and shuffling in her crate,
and you there waiting for me,
better self, mother, grief,
you who were missing the whole day
while I sat being productive.

3.

The bath runs. I take painkillers.
I'm not sure which pain I need them for.
You said when I stopped drinking,
I started to be boring.

If I had to live alone again,
I don't know if I could cope
with the loneliness. I don't know
if God would provide.

At the table of the narcissists I sat down to eat.
They ate wolfishly, alert to every slight
as they bared their teeth.

Today is a green water day.
I'm tired of putting things into lines.
I just want to rest.

Units

1.

It's autumn in La Chaux-de-Fonds.
The last day of August, the mists arriving early,
everyone in anoraks.
10.30 a.m. and already we're drinking.
We won't be together like this again,
not here, not anywhere.
It's autumn in La Chaux-de-Fonds.
We climb up out of the town, past the stadium,
and into more mist. There's a fire. Smoke in the trees.
Hard to tell where smoke ends, cloud begins.
On the path back to the cars we look across the gorge
into the next country. More cars go screaming
up and down the Pod into the small hours.

2.

I've never had an 'off' switch around alcohol.
I can look at a sealed bottle for weeks
but once it's open, game over.
When I was about fourteen, I'd sneak off
to the larder under the stairs and take gulps
of my father's cider straight from the bottle.
I loved the sweetness, the gentle fizz.
It made me feel bolder, fuller.
A slight burning sensation in my nostrils.
The feeling of confidence that school said I needed.
The nearest I came to hanging onto it
when I stepped on stage.
A safely minor role at first, then speaking parts,
a middle-class woman, a scientist in an absurdist satire
about a man with a tiger in his bathroom.
I could make an audience gasp.
My shock at that. My need for it.
The silence after they went home,
toasting myself in the mirror.

Call Me

We play message tennis.
I get to Tuesday
and put it off till Friday
then forget.

The weekend, I say.
Then that goes, exactly where
I'm not sure.
Maybe Monday.

I wasn't there when she died
and only a visitor as she faded.
I'm not a good sibling
or son.

Wall

I've hit the wall, Hubert.
I've been taking your poems
with me through it and into it
to see if poetry can stand up
to experience like we say it does.

My mother died and work
got too much and now your poems,
their riddling columns of thirteen lines
weaving in and out of me.
Should I attach myself

to these thoughts,
memories and feelings,
so many of them from the past?
While she was dying
all I talked about was school.

You are through the wall with me
in this raw place
where I breathe and breathe
and remember that to stand up
sometimes you have to fall.

You Were Good

You were good,
though difficult,
and now you're gone.

Mostly I knew fear
near you,
though you were good.

Now you're gone
your fear has, too,
which is good.

When we made peace
you held my hand.
You told me I was good.

You were good.
And difficult.

Mother/Son

1.

You sat beneath my window
in early October
sunlight speaking
French with Michèle
like you had all
the time
in the world
which you did then
the hottest October day
since records
began
a record broken
so many times since
it's hard to remember
the shock of it happening
the first time

2.

You told me I had to change
out of my shorts
for church
and when I asked why
you told me my legs were beautiful
not covering them might stop others
worshipping
and when I said how
you told me my beauty
might be distracting
and when I asked what beauty
you said

> *your beauty*
> *your legs*
> *you are beautiful*
> *which is distracting*

3.

You were frightened of Shakespeare
but loved dressing up for the theatre
so were happy
to see Dustin Hoffman as Shylock
and Zoë Wanamaker as Viola
even though none of it made sense
except when Daddy clapped
in the wrong place
because he was so moved
and you took his hand
in the silent auditorium
and that was all
that needed saying

4.

You were the only one in your family
everyone got on with —
even Coucou when he was raging
or Michèle's unreachable tears

you knew a way of talking
to each which tricked them human —
though panicked by their anger or loss
some seas of the same rising in you also

but meeting theirs with words
they could hear and meet themselves
coming back from wherever they'd gone to

and you would embrace them
or put the phone down
in the kitchen
and come back to us

and start again
because you had to

5.

You were first to read my poems
a stash of them in small
plain A5 notebooks
reporter style
kept in my bedside table

the shock of you
looking without asking
the words coming
out of your mouth —

> *you must*
> *keep writing*
> *Anthony it's*
> *you are so clever*
> *I had no*
> *you had such deep*
> *I had no*
> *idea*

you burgled me
to say this —

> *no idea*
> *such deep*
> *keep writing*

6.

You told me once the only thing
you remembered
from your schooling
was a single sentence
of Latin —

    sunt formicis parvis animalibus

then (you said)
your mother
fell ill
and you left
to look after
the family

    I was sixteen I
    made the best
    of it because
    in those days
    that was how
    it worked

7.

You prayed long graces
right into the heart of it
when it had all but eaten
you up
the insatiable beast of it gobbling
you daily —
but not this

> *Father God*
> *we thank you*
> *for all the good things*
> *you give to us*
> *and we remember*
> *all the good things*
> *and those who do not have enough*
> *you are so good*
> *and we bless you*

and then from somewhere
that nothing could touch
your grandchildren
each of them
by name

8.

You compared us with other boys
from church —
they were better behaved
talked less
and didn't drop their pencils

(walking past the gates
   of the campus today
      I glimpsed
         the quad now overrun
            with wildflowers flashing yellow)

the sermons wore on
past the moment anyone cared
where on earth they started

(in the sunshine)

a perfect place for a picnic
let's sit down and eat

9.

You told your Bible Study Group
you cried when homeless people begged
you for money

and you cried again when they persuaded
you never to give in and follow
your instinct
to share what you had

it burned you and in you
your heart
where they couldn't see

even as they lowered their heads
to pray saying
let's give this to God

Hymn of Rain

The quality of mercy?
You must be joking.
I begin as *ice*.
I come as veil or wraith,
a whisper of Spanish lace.

I sleep in your bones, your bed.
I leak from your pores,
the spittle of your snores.
I keep you indoors.

I'm a smirr, I'm a smudge,
I'm a smattering
of all you find frightening.

I'm a mudslide
but you don't know about that.
I bring thoughts of holidays,
wet childhoods, wellington boots.

I'm a drum, I'm a siren,
I'm an orphanage.
I'm the remnants of a village
clinging to a straw roof.

I have plans for everyone.
Yes, even the desert.
How would you like that —
to see even the barren places mirror sky?

Do you know I am coming?
(You know.)

All There

Were we all there once?
When was that,
that time?

It rained, the sun shone,
that picnic with the cows.
How we laughed!

A long time. A long time.
Were you there?
Weren't we all there?

The willows
in the river.
That kingfisher.

Long, long laughter.
Where was it when we.
Where did we go?

Truce

Who gave the order,
no one knew.
They say there wasn't one.

Stille Nacht in no man's,
its accordion leaking like gas
across the frost.

One by one came stars,
better to pick out
white rags.

What I remember next
is nothing
(if absence

is what nothing is), a song
into which we sang silence.
Witnesses,

we witnessed it.
We were part of that cloud,
and lost in it.

The Divide

The way the world divides
(the red and blue
halves of a city taking sides)
could be me and you.

The way I apologise
for looking through
and not into your eyes
is not exactly new.

Nor the way you itemise
my idiotic views,
the way my pride
stops short at 'love' and 'you'.

Fury

I'm watching the Branagh-Wallanders in order.
Their atmosphere brooding, oddly poetic.
Each series took six months to film.
It's not until the middle of the second
that we see him wake up in a bed –
an armchair, his office, even a dead colleague's sofa.

When we stayed on the archipelago,
the welcome pack told us
that half the households in Sweden
possess a box set of *Midsomer Murders*.
All that home counties restraint
and thatched cottage fury is exotic after all.

I loved the Krister Henriksson versions too,
but even those are starting to fade for me now.
All I remember is his house by the sea
and an image of him watching his daughter
windsurfing after solving an especially brutal case
involving the trafficking of sex workers.

The Small Rain

i

The rain's a lost child
wandering the zoo

at midnight
with only wolves for company.

At dawn they slink
back inside —

the light
has nothing to teach them.

The rain isn't bothered.
A wet wolf is

a wet hyena
a child crying.

The new anguish
is like the old anguish.

Just as raw
but with a better sound system.

ii

The rain's a kind of memory
cleansing the roads
of leaves
tiny stones
the bones of dead foxes.

The fields have nothing to say
merely shrugging
in the downpour
the better
to get it over with.

iii

Piano notes
arrange themselves

with help
from you

playing them
in twos

and threes
then pause

before finding
voice again

in twos
and threes

fresher than
before and

exactly the
same except

you played
them not

knowing what
came next

To the Wife of a Famous Poet

When you accosted me
at the conference

and shouted my name
(though I stood one pace from your mouth)

into the air,
declaring it a

useless
name for a poet,

what poisonous motivations
thickened in your veins,

what certainties,
that my name, which you brayed

with such glee,
my name,

which you branded useless,
could never match that

of your husband,
guardian of tradition and canon,

protector of excellence,
name I learnt as a schoolboy,

name of less uselessness than mine,
name of more than consequence,

a name one could drop,
as you did, before you cursed

my name,
declaring it useless?

The Gift of Tongues

The shit-shower-shave, the curry, the vid,
the three-day rave, the opening bid,
the stark-bollock-naked, the stag, the twist,
the opening gambit, the drift, the gist.

The three-wickets-down, the leading edge,
the going-to-ground, the nod, the hedge,
the belter, the craic, the post-wedding sesh,
the midsummer madness, the anyone's-guess.

The who-gives-a-toss, the under-the-bar,
the being-the-boss, the who-we-all-are,
the what-it's-all-for, the heave, the lift,
the reason we do it, the moment, the gift.

Sorry

When I speak to her
and meet with him
and see the damage you did
I'm sorry I got you.

I'm sorry to have to say this
and I still love you but
I'm sorry I got you when
we divided the spoils.

When I look at them
and when I look at you
I wonder which side I'm on.
It seems that I got you,
and I'm sorry.

With Hey, Ho, the Wind and the Rain

i

When the rain came looking for me
I hid.

I felt myself a child.
I felt myself apprehend

what it meant
to finally leave home.

The rain wasn't interested.
When I came out of hiding

it was still raining.
My childhood my only company.

It is still raining.
I am still dancing.

I am all
memory.

ii

The rain is keeping us prisoner.
It takes even longer to die

than Wolverine in *Logan*
('So this is what it's like').

The rain's on the news every night
but for the wrong reasons.

So British, so Dunkirk,
so Cat Up Tree.

This is late period *Poirot*
everyone assembled in the drawing room

the bitter uncles and spinster aunts
living off their repeat fees

with no idea who did it
until the final moment

by which time
it's too late

even for the young couple
driving off into the sunset

with eyes only for each other
and who speak of falling in love

as though
they invented it.

iii

During my creativity lecture
in which not one soul

had heard of Joni Mitchell
it was raining.

I tried to stop my eyes rolling
but years of micro-aggressions

on pay and conditions
have taken their toll.

This isn't statistical.

The theatre was a sauna.
(There's a soya option now for *lattes*.)

I thought of the woman I met
at the teach-out who said

she'd been told what to think
her whole life. She'd 'probably

do a Masters' just in case.
It was raining then too.

Who's to say which of us noticed?
We filed into it

full of flapjack,
our collars erect with knowledge.

In humans vs physics
physics always wins.

iv

When I began writing
about rain

forty-seven poems ago
I'd no idea

it would take over
my life.

What was it my therapist said?
To move on

you need to stop boxing
things up.

I won't say I've enjoyed it
but it's been fun.

I don't care that Hospitality Services vans
are electric and silent.

I just want to stop crying
as I come on to campus.

Plus a library that has staff.
With such threads

do we make our tapestry of rain.
Either everything's a poem

or nothing is.

Old School

'Don't forget, this is inside us every day.'
—STEPHEN BERG

1. Mawer

An Oxford rowing blue, his only interests were the river & the quartet of Labradors in the back of his Volvo. Smoked a pipe during lunch while the dogs roamed the quad. Intensely lazy. Wrote on my maths homework *Only a gentleman uses black ink*. Rumours of a marriage, but no. Saw he'd died recently in the school magazine they insist on sending with requests for money (an art or language block here, a boathouse there). The most bored human I ever met. We were a way of passing the time while he daydreamed about river-mist and dogs.

2. Steggles

An enormous man, pompous beyond belief but not without self-awareness and humour. Taught bottom-set maths to the most senior boys, each of us a captain or prefect of something. Otherwise, gods. A miracle how he got us to leave our pride, insecurity & shame at the door. When I visited he'd shrunk. You could see the man inside the man. I thanked him with a handshake like the leper in the story. Don't think he remembered me. Heard he went to South Africa to be a missionary, shrank even more & was much loved. Crowd of three hundred when he died.

3. Spin

Taught my father after the war (must have been young then) & stayed at the same school for 30+ years, popping out for a gasper between lessons in his pale grey suit (thought we couldn't see him). A genius. Struggled when confronted with non-genius. Worked out the timetable during his summer holidays (for fun!) while his mother brought scrambled eggs he never touched. Our one conversation — called me 'polytechnic material'. Suggested teaching because he was bored (nothing else came to mind). Looked at me uncomprehendingly, like when I failed maths for the third time. All those November afternoons with the bottom set, the eggs he stubbed out in, his life's work on the back of an envelope.

4. *Speller*

It's June in chapel when Speller loses it. His arms spring from his sides as though released from a straitjacket. He's swinging himself off the end of an invisible trapeze, high above us, whole body arched. The plastic ruler gripped between his forefinger & thumb swings out & back. His legs have gone to jelly at the knees. He's a clown doing the twist, hips swivelling towards the floor. Almost at the point of no return, he springs back on tiptoe, ruler swinging. His geometry tin crashes to the floor, pens & pencils scuttling out of sight. After the exam, we find him in T-shirt & jeans playing tennis against the chapel wall. *Larkin was wrong about boredom!* he shouts. He spits a backhand, eyes wild. The ball catches the rim of his racket & spins high, arcing towards the roof. His eyes don't follow. He only has eyes for the wall.

5. Gauntlet

i.

Yaffle stuck his head out of the Old Hall door and the ruckus came to a halt. I had just been flung-shoved, kicked and punched on the way, by boys from the year above who lined the corridor outside and whose gauntlet this was every Friday after Geography. Yaffle gave a sniff, ducked back in and the ruckus continued.

ii.

The fight scenes in *West Side Story* were actual fights, Stuart Frame landing blows on my face and head as he sprang unseen from the wings. Why I agreed to pair with him I don't know. How he loved unleashing mayhem without punishment in plain sight.

iii.

Neil Waller grabbed my lapels and threw me down the back stairs of the Dining Hall. Feet away louche prefects leant on the door jamb and pretended not to hear the sound of boys landing, helped by kicks and fists of lesser bullies, at the foot of the concrete steps.

6. The Dining Hall

The missionary boards frowned down on us while we ate. Harvey-Jones, 1923, India. There was a lot of India, quite a lot of Africa & China too. Ceylon. Remember the old dining hall joke? The dog food they served us: was it *for* dogs or made of them? Eventually the missionaries died off. Featherstonehaugh, 1975, Zaire. Then silence.

That's where I eat before I give my reading. The boards have gone. Light everywhere. A salad bar. A three-bean panini. The staff charming. No more Broadbent. No more God looking the other way while he did it. No one calling you cunt.

In Late Rainy Season

Like good boys and girls, we attended church
regularly, where we learned that God was for us,
not against us. It was unseasonably wet, causing
sneezes and coughs to ripple among the pews
like the germ of an idea that hadn't yet been tested
in the fire of open discussion. God was for us,
not against us, except for those He targeted
with His anger. Luckily, we weren't among them,
so skipped towards home without looking back,
only pausing to marvel at His creation, which sang
and rejoiced at marvels to which we were also blind.

It Raineth

i.

I can't do this any more.
Each day I walk into the rain

and each day I get lost in it.
I can't feel my hands.

Shame, on the other hand —
now you're talking.

Who knew there was so much
to be found in a half-rhyme

this innocent afternoon
in late February?

The funerals come,
the funerals go.

On the way
(and back)

there's rain.
There'll be an afterlife

I'm sure of it.
If there *is* one

please God
go easy on the rainbows.

ii.

The rain falls on Northwood.
My mother watches it as snow

remembering the waist-deep snow
of her childhood

not this suburban nonsense
already melting in the rain.

Steady now and intricate.
Completely consistent on its own terms.

Wherever your loss is located
the terms are the same —

La Chaux-de-Fonds, Renens,
Neuchâtel, Pully —

even Northwood
stripes emerging on the lawn

from beneath melting snow
like a memory returning.

*Oh, it's you, I like you,
have you been here before?*

iii.

Heaney loved the rain.
Kennelly too. Even Beckett.

'Its low conducive voices'
(one hundred days

in a row now)
have done my head

in.
At Mary's funeral

I went for 'The Good'.
I needed sunshine.

Need it. To shine.
Which it did, that day.

I have spent my life
trying to impress

somebody —
nearly always the wrong person.

And down it comes.
Inscrutable. Freezing.
Unrepentant.

Soon I must go out in it.
When I stroked the small of your back

and later when we slept
it was still raining.

Bowled

I end the year as I began it, wearing old clothes
and trying to concentrate on a Wallander novel.
Stop being a poet, a friend said,
by which I took to mean the peripheral nonsense
I'd filled my life with. So I did. It was so easy!
I read four poets and gave up on two of them,
one of whom went on to win the Nobel
six months later. (No accounting for taste.)
The other was Donne.
I'm still 'seventeen, skinny, dissatisfied' in front of him,
his eyes bearing down on me. My mother
has yet to discover my poems
and I'm at the peak of my popularity at school —
though not among the praying classes:
they demand I be torn off a strip by the Head
for my role in the school play, I'm the spawn of Satan
(I bond with the English teachers, after all).
I celebrate by bowling the cricket master in the staff match,
which we lose on the last ball.
Cricket will always appear in my work.
Cricket will always appear in my work.
But this isn't about cricket, this is about death.

Illusion IV (part of a series)

The Dean is not an ogre.
For one thing, he is a City fan.

We spend our lives
decoding his emails

when all we need to do
is look at his art.

I'm not saying it's bad,
just that it should be burned.

The time we met
(the other I tabled a question)

I said 'Nice art',
which makes me the liar, not him.

He is amazingly consistent:
work harder or you're out.

I can live with that.
He did not ask to become the symbol

of our self-hatred,
our fears about elegance of ideas

no longer being the point
of what we write.

What he knows, he tells us.
The world runs on money, not poems.

All is Lost (Spoiler Alert)

Robert Redford watches his boat disappear
in the middle of the ocean

certain he is going to die
in the wettest film ever made.

Incredible to think
his specs somehow make it

into the emergency kit
along with stationery.

His opening line (VO, credits) –
'I'm sorry' –

what the whole thing
takes to unravel.

Let me save you the time.
In the end a hand

comes down to save him
(third container ship lucky)

but not until after he sets fire
to his life raft

and gives in to the black depths
with a burble.

Choose your own metaphor.
I actually thought he'd bought it

and was happy
(if happy is the right word)

with the decision
much more than *The Perfect Storm*

which I made the mistake of watching
after I got better

and which
unlike everything else I have loved

I still regret
not reading up on first.

Now and Not Yet

We are in Tesco in Exeter
waiting for a funeral.

These dried pink and rubber things
are scrambled eggs, salmon and a bagel.

In Cascais our taxi driver
described Paula Rego as *a very strange woman.*

The gallery
served the darkest coffee of the trip.

When I told you I did not care
you hated my music

I lied. I've been doing it
my whole life.

From Christmas madness
to one violin

in an empty kitchen
we go on crying

because we go on
loving you.

On the Nature of Daylight

Three nights in a row now
sleep severed from me

thoughts a fairground
at the edge of town

which colonise
everything.

I did not vote
to die poorer

but the rain
insists that I did.

It could be worse.
I could be Kenneth Branagh

raging in a field
clothes whirling about him

his daughter
a stranger.

Instead, this is England
in bright downpour.

As the credits to *Arrival*
disappeared

up the screen
I understood everything

in a language
I am not prepared to learn.

Toast

September and still warm.
Concentration in pieces.

The shame-dreams come,
the shame-dreams go,
always the same, with
different teachers speaking.

You see it coming, you see it
but you don't see it coming.
I bury myself in the bedclothes,
my words turning over.

Did I say enough? My shoulders
no longer remember.

Lines lost in the small hours.

Toast then more toast. My eyes
rinse themselves in the dark.

I Mean to Call Daddy

but he calls instead
cheery as ever.

I have not lost
a life partner.

But here he is
asking me how I am.

Fine, I say.
(I'm not.)

How are you?
He's not fine either.

Instead
we talk about rugby

the weather
like when I phoned from school.

Piste Vita

The saddest thing I ever saw
was your body

remembering
how to slalom

in front of *Ski Sunday*.
You completed your warm-up

on time
(you were always on time)

ready
to plunge

downhill
safe in the knowledge

you would cross the finish line
first

even though you had no idea
where you were going

except that it ended
in snow.

Acknowledgements

Acknowledgements and thanks are due to the editors of the following where versions of these poems first appeared: *Ambit, Anthropocene, Atrium, Butcher's Dog, Exeter Flying Post, The Friday Poem, Ink Sweat & Tears, The Interpreter's House, London Grip, Moist, The North, The Rialto, Riptide, Stride, Under the Radar, USS Briefs.*

'Wall' is for Hubert Moore.

'The Gift of Tongues' is for Peter Carpenter.

The lines of Raymond Carver used in 'After Raymond Carver' are from 'Happiness', *In a Marine Light: Selected Poems* (Picador, 1988).

The lines of Seamus Heaney used in 'It Raineth' are from 'Exposure', *North* (Faber and Faber Ltd, 1975).

The lines of Thom Gunn used in 'Bowled' are from 'Autobiography', *Selected Poems*, edited by Clive Wilmer (Faber and Faber Ltd, 2017).

I acknowledge a debt of influence to Lucille Clifton, Robert Rehder and Toon Tellegen in the composition of some of these poems.

Thank you, Rob Mackenzie

For cheering me on in the dark times, thank you, Amy Shelton, Ann Sansom, Andrew Rumsey, Colin Mallett, Gwenllian Riall, Jim Harris, John Foggin, Kester Brewin, Louis de Pelet, Lucy Runge, Luke Bretherton, Martin Wroe, Peter Sansom, Rachel Griffiths, Rebecca de Pelet, and Shawna Lemay.

Thank you, Christopher Southgate.
Thank you, Ann Gray, Hilary Menos, Sally Flint.
Thank you, Josephine Corcoran.
Thank you, Michael Symmons Roberts.
Thank you, Sue Dymoke, Cliff Yates, Michael Laskey, Hubert Moore.
Thank you, Maura Dooley.
Thank you, Peter Carpenter.
Thank you, Helena Nelson, for your editing, advice, wisdom and patience.

Anthony Wilson is a poet, writing tutor and lecturer. He works in medical and teacher education at the University of Exeter.

The Wind and the Rain is his sixth collection of poetry. His memoir of cancer, *Love for Now* (Impress Books), was published in 2012. He is also the author of *Deck Shoes* (Impress Books, 2019), a collection of essays and criticism.

In 2015, he published the best-selling anthology *Lifesaving Poems* with Bloodaxe Books, based on his blog of the same name.

www.anthonywilsonpoetry.com